GROW
Deepen Your Relationship with Christ

Joel Comiskey

Published by CCS Publishing

CCS Publishing

www.joelcomiskeygroup.com

Published by CCS Publishing
23890 Brittlebush Circle
Moreno Valley, CA 92557 USA
1-888-344-CELL

Third printing, December 2008

Cover design by Josh Talbot
Editing by Scott Boren

CCS Publishing is the book-publishing division of Cell Church Solutions, a resource and coaching ministry dedicated to equipping leaders for cell-based ministry. Find us on the World Wide Web at **www.joelcomiskeygroup.com**

Publisher's Cataloging-in-Publication
  (Provided by Quality Books, Inc.)

Comiskey, Joel, 1956-
   Grow: deepen your relationship with Christ / by
Joel Comiskey.
   p. cm.
   Includes bibliographical references and index.
   ISBN 0975581937

   1. Spiritual life--Christianity. 2. Meditation--
Christianity. 3. Spiritual formation.   I. Title.

BV4501.3.C6553 2007   248.4
                    QBI06-600331

Table of Contents

Introduction

I often tell people, "After receiving Jesus and being filled with the Spirit, the daily quiet time is the most important part of the Christian life." I believe this with all my heart.

During the quiet time a Christian learns to feed from God's Word, hear His voice, and find daily strength.

I view my daily quiet time as my lifeline with the living God and the most important feature of my Christian life. I grow in intimacy with my Lord and Savior during my quiet time. He also shows me how to live, what appointments to keep or cancel, and what's important in life. It's like spending time in the presence of the person you love.

I strongly believe in the book you are about to study.

If you're working through this book alone, you would benefit from meeting with a coach who can work with you, answer your questions, and hold you accountable. In the appendix, you'll find tips for coaches.

Additional resources

Grow is part of a five-book series that prepares someone to become a mature follower of Jesus Christ. The goal of this book is to teach you how to spend quality time with God.

If you are interested in the other four books in this series, you can purchase them at www.joelcomiskeygroup.com or by calling 1-888-344-CELL. Along with *Grow,* I recommend that you read my book *An Appointment with the King,* which can be purchased on the web site or by calling the toll free number.

You can use this book individually, in a small group setting, or in a classroom. Many churches will teach this material in a group setting. This is the normal way to teach the material, but it's only one way. I've provided teaching outlines and PowerPoints for all five equipping books in this series on a CD. This CD can be purchased at the CCS web site or toll free number

Connecting with God

I n 1989, my wife Celyce and I, newly married, were on our way home from a church service in Escondido, California. Just as darkness descended upon a deserted stretch of Interstate Freeway 15, our old Toyota sputtered to a stop. Out of gas. I was busy that week and had forgotten to fill the tank. There were no telephones, no houses, nothing nearby. I opened the car door shocked by our bleak circumstances. "I guess I'll just have to put out my thumb," I mumbled to myself.

Within three minutes, a smiling person stopped, introduced himself as a Christian evangelist, drove us to the nearest gas station (many miles away) and back again to the car. Unforgettable. A miracle straight from the throne of God—yet I dare not tempt God again by purposely running out of gas on a dark highway just to see if another evangelist, or perhaps an apostle, would stop!

Just as cars run out of gas, so do Christians stop functioning spiritually unless they receive fuel from above. As a believer you will have little impact on others if you are running on empty. Daily quiet time with God provides the spiritual sustenance necessary to fill up our souls.

A daily connection

The quiet time is an activity that takes place at a certain time and a certain place on a daily basis. It's a time set aside to read the Bible, pray, and seek God.

What is the Scriptural evidence for a daily quiet time? While there are many implied references in the Bible, the main one is Matthew 6:6: "But when you pray, go into your room, close the door and pray to your Father, who is unseen. Then your Father, who sees what is done in secret, will reward you."

In this verse, Jesus talks about a specific time ("when") and a specific place ("room") to spend time with the God who sees what is done in secret. God wants us to connect with Him on a daily basis at a particular place and time.

Try IT!

Read Matthew 6:5.
How did the hypocrites pray?

_____

_____

_____

Why does God dislike this way of praying? How can you avoid it?

_____

_____

_____

_____

_____

_____

Two ways of connecting with God

Paul says in 1 Thessalonians 5:17, "pray continually; give thanks in all circumstances, for this is God's will for you in Christ Jesus." It's very important that we talk to God throughout the day. The Bible tells us to pray all the time. Praying throughout the day, however, shouldn't be a substitute for spending daily time with God in a specific place and at a specific time. You'll notice in the box below the differences between having a set devotional time and praying continually.

| Quiet time versus praying continually ||
Quiet time	Praying continually
• Receiving God's fullness	• Maintaining God's fullness
• Studying God's Word	• Remembering God's Word
• Waiting on God	• Walking with God
• Praying about particular matters	• Praying moment by moment

Quiet time and praying continually feed each other and are both important. Personal time with God refreshes and empowers us to walk in the Spirit for the rest of the day. After spending time in His presence, you will notice a new sensitivity to God in your daily activities. Praying without ceasing is the afterglow of receiving God's abundance in our quiet time. Just don't make the mistake of substituting one for the other.

What do you actually do during the quiet time?

When I first started dating Celyce, I would plan our dates to make sure everything was perfect. I decided where we should go and what we should do. Yet, during the date, our conversation flowed naturally. I didn't bring a script or set of notes to guide our conversation. Our interaction flowed in a free, spontaneous way.

I do believe that certain guidelines about what to do in the quiet time (e.g., Bible reading plans, how to pray, etc.) are helpful. Yet, ultimately, the goal of the quiet time is to know God in a more intimate way. Just as the flow of conversation with Celyce was natural and spontaneous, so also what takes place in the quiet time should be flexible and spontaneous. The goal is to develop a relationship with the living God. The apostle Paul said in Philippians 3:10–11, "I want to know Christ and the power of his resurrection and the fellowship of sharing in his sufferings, becoming like him in his death and so, somehow, to attain to the resurrection from the dead."

We get to know God by reading His Word, listening to His voice, worshipping, praying, and practicing spiritual disciplines. These areas will be covered in following chapters of this book.

Many people look at the quiet time as rules to keep, rather than a relationship to have with the living God. This is not true! The quiet time is all about getting to know God on an intimate level and enjoying that wonderful fellowship with Him on a continual basis.

Try IT!

Read John 17:3.
How did Jesus describe eternal life?

_____

_____

_____

How can you make knowing God your principal goal?

_____

_____

_____

_____

_____

_____

Why spend daily time with God?

God desires to spend time with us more than we want to spend with Him. In fact, he made us with the desire to spend time with Him. We pursue God because He first pursued us; He places the desire in our hearts. And it's that desire that will sustain you day after day.

The good news is that as you spend time with God, the desire to be with Him will grow.

Try IT!

Read Romans 8:28–39.
What is God's attitude toward His children?

_____

_____

_____

How can you apply these verses in your own life?

_____

_____

_____

_____

_____

_____

_____

The Bible says, "We love him because HE first loved us" (1 John 4:10). It's God's rich love that stirs us to seek Him every day. Spending time with Him each day is when we delight in His goodness and thank Him for all He's done and will do.

And the amazing thing is that God wants to spend time with us more than we want to spend time with Him. He knows we need Him more than we understand our own need.

Daily strength

We need to spend time with God because we need daily strength. Jesus said, "Therefore do not worry about tomorrow, for tomorrow will worry about itself. Each day has enough trouble of its own" (Matthew 6:34). Because we face new challenges each day, we can't depend on yesterday's encounter with God. We need strength each day, and the quiet time helps us to prepare for the daily challenges of life, as we allow God to lead us to victory.

Try IT!

What are some of your daily struggles?

_____

_____

_____

_____

How can the quiet time help you to face those things?

_____

_____

_____

_____

_____

_____

_____

Some people substitute going to church for the quiet time. While attending church helps believers grow and is vital to the Christian life, it's no substitute for daily time with Jesus. We need to understand how to feed ourselves.

Just as we need daily physical food, so also we need daily spiritual food. Jesus addressed this issue in Matthew 6:11 where it says, "Give us today our daily bread." You'll notice the word daily. Our human bodies are designed to eat daily. Our spiritual lives also need daily strength and vibrancy. We receive this daily bread through reading God's Word, meditating on specific Scripture, worshiping, listening to God, confessing sin, and prayer.

Try IT!

Read Matthew 6:34.
What does this verse tell us to avoid?

_____

_____

_____

How can you apply this verse to your current situation?

_____

_____

_____

_____

_____

_____

_____

Do IT!
Commit yourself to start have a daily quiet time this week.

God's reward

You'll notice that Matthew 6:6 includes a reward. Jesus said, "But when you pray, go into your room, close the door and pray to your Father, who is unseen. Then your Father, who sees what is done in secret, will reward you." God will bless your life and prosper you in many different ways. God is the One who rewards those who seek Him in secret.

Try IT!

Matthew 6:6 mentions a reward.
How do you hope to see God's reward in your own life?

_____

_____

_____

_____

_____

_____

Personally, God often blesses me in my quiet time by showing me how to manage my life. I'll be praying and suddenly He'll show me how to arrange my schedule so I can get the most done in my day and week. Or He'll show me how to communicate more effectively with my wife, daughters, or business associates. So often God rewards us in those areas we might consider mundane. It's not a flash of lightening, or a miraculous touch that is God's normal way of speaking to us in the quiet time.

Try IT!

True or false:
- ☐ A quiet time helps us grow.
- ☐ A quiet time helps us earn merit so we can go to heaven.
- ☐ A quiet time strengthens our relationship with God.

I've discovered an inverse equation about spending time with God. If you make spending time with God your top priority, He will help you get more accomplished during the day. Martin Luther once said during an especially busy time, "I have so much to do today that I should spend the first three hours in prayer."

Memorize IT!
Matthew 6:6: "But when you pray, go into your room, close the door and pray to your Father, who is unseen. Then your Father, who sees what is done in secret, will reward you."

Remember IT!

What had the most impact for you in this lesson?

_____

_____

_____

_____

_____

_____

_____

Main points:
1. Quiet time empowers us to walk in the Spirit and "pray continually" throughout the rest of the day.
2. There is no one set way to have a quiet time. The important thing is to draw close to God, thus avoiding ritual and routine.
3. We need to spend daily time with God in order to receive regular spiritual nourishment.

Apply IT!

1. Of all the reasons for spending time with God, which do you find is most important to you? Why?
2. What is the main reason to have the quiet time?
3. What obstacles in your quiet time keep you from getting closer to God?
4. Block off time for an appointment with God each day for the next week.

Preparing to Meet God

You are in the White House waiting to meet the president of the United States. In five minutes it will be your turn to shake his hand and see the Oval Office, the dream of a lifetime. You're nervous, over prepared, yet hoping to appear relaxed. Then you see the door swing open and hear the words, "Please come in."

Now picture this. The King of Kings, far more important than any worldly dignitary, has requested your presence. He's invited you to appear before His majestic throne room. And He's not interested in a "photo op" or a one-time handshake—He wants to meet with you everyday.

Placing God-time in the schedule

Jesus made it a priority when He was on earth to spend time alone with His Father. In fact, the busier Jesus was, the more time He needed to be with the Father. Luke 5:15 explains that as Jesus' fame spread, the success of His ministry compelled Him to spend more time with God. Verse 16 says, "Jesus often withdrew to lonely places and prayed." In the midst of an increasingly busy ministry, He separated from the multitude for a quiet time. If Jesus, God's Son and our model, spent His time with the Father, shouldn't we? The answer is of course we need to spend time with God. But when?

Choosing the best time

I think the best time is when you are the most awake. Some people, believe it or not, are at the height of their mental powers in the evening. These same people accomplish little in the morning—

including spending time with God. And since God deserves our best time, such people should have their quiet time in the evening.

Try IT!

Read Psalm 5:3.
When does the writer of this Psalm approach God?

_____

_____

What are the benefits of the morning for you?

_____

_____

_____

_____

_____

_____

_____

_____

Another factor is the best schedule. Mothers with small children might decide to have their quiet time during naptime, mid-morning, or in the afternoon. A freeway commuter might decide that the best time is at 12 noon in the quiet of his or her office. Alertness and time availability are key factors in deciding on the quiet time.

Jesus often chose the morning hour to seek God. Mark 1:35 says, "Very early in the morning, while it was still dark, Jesus got up, left the house and went off to a solitary place, where he prayed." One important aspect of the morning quiet time is that your mind is fresh. A night's rest empowers most people to think more clearly. Can you think of other positive reasons for having a quiet time in the morning? Others prefer the afternoon or evening because they are more awake, have more time, or concentrate better.

If you choose the evening, it gives you a chance to reflect on your day in light of Scripture, and to prepare yourself for the following day's battle. In addition, people who spend daily time with God in the evening say they sleep more peacefully because they have placed the burdens of the day at the Father's feet.

Try IT!

Does morning, afternoon, or evening best fit your schedule to have a quiet time? Why?

_____

_____

_____

_____

_____

_____

_____

_____

Be consistent

Lack of consistency is probably the greatest hindrance to regular, daily quiet time. I've asked some people how often they have quiet times and they responded, "When I feel like it." The problem with this answer is that when people don't feel like it, they don't have it. Over time, you develop the habit of not having a daily quiet time. You don't have to "feel like it" to have daily devotions. Quiet time is a matter of faith and discipline--not feelings.

Determine that your quiet time will be the first thing you put on your schedule. It's an appointment with the King! Everett Lewis Cattell, a Mennonite pastor in the 1960s, says, "There must be regularity of time ... in order merely to guarantee that we get at it and get it done. Fortunately, this leads to better things as the discipline gives way to joy."[1]

I recommend several keys to be consistent in your quiet time:

1. Set a time. The likelihood that you'll actually have a quiet time will increase when you actually put it in your schedule.
2. Plan your daily activity around the time you set. You need to plan your schedule around your quiet time rather than the other way around.
3. Set the amount of time you're going to spend with God. I recommend starting with one-half hour and graduating to one hour.
4. Stick with it. At first you might only get five minutes of quality time. But as you stick with it, that five minutes will turn into 20 and 30 minutes and your time with God will be the greatest delight in your day.
5. Above all, remember that the goal is to get to know the living God. The quiet time is all about relationship. It's getting to know your best friend.

---

1. Everett Lewis Cattell, *The Spirit of Holiness* (Kansas City, Mo.: Beacon Hill, 1963), 64.

Try IT!

Of the above five suggestions on the opposite page, which one is the most helpful in your situation right now? Why?

_____

_____

_____

_____

_____

_____

_____

_____

_____

_____

_____

Accept failures

Spending time with God should be a delight, not a burden. It's communion with the King, not a ritualistic activity that you have to fulfill to avoid feelings of guilt and failure. Thus, when circumstances dictate that you can't spend time with God, don't let the devil condemn you. Yes, you will fail. Circumstances will arise when it will be very difficult to keep your normal schedule. Take those exceptions in stride and don't give up. The thesis of this book is to make your quiet time the daily rule of your life. Of course, exceptions to that rule will occur. That's part of life.

How much time to spend with God

Having a daily quiet time is like running a marathon race, not the fifty-yard dash. Many start well only to fizzle out later. They expected too much of themselves in the beginning. Don't try to be a spiritual giant in one leap of faith. God will reveal how much time He wants you to spend with Him each day. You do not need to give up your job and family and spend eight hours each day in prayer. Set a realistic goal you can keep, rather than one you're sure to break.

Try IT!

In your opinion, how much time should a person spend in his or her daily quiet time?

_____

_____

_____

_____

_____

_____

_____

_____

Finding a balance

I remember reading about past Christian heroes who would spend five to six hours each day in personal prayer. I then tried to find five extra hours in my day for prayer. Most days I failed miserably. I'll never forget a friend waking me up in the prayer room when I had been in there for hours. For those starting their journey in spending time with God, there is the danger of trying to spend too much time with Him. When your zeal wears thin, you might feel burned out and stop having quiet times altogether. The devil would love nothing more.

A more common problem in today's fast-paced society is not spending enough time with God. Many want spiritual progress without paying the price for that growth. Growth in intimacy with the living God takes time. Without doubt, it does take time to lay aside the busy, worrisome thoughts of the day. If you don't linger in God's presence, you probably won't find His joy and peace. Don't rob yourself of God's blessing by leaving His presence when He's about to fill you. It might only take ten minutes to order, eat, and leave at McDonalds, but that won't work during the quiet time. Granted, ten minutes is better than zero minutes. But thirty minutes allows breathing room and opens the door for communion with God.

Memorize IT!
Matthew 6:33: "But seek first his kingdom and his righteousness, and all these things will be given to you as well."

Amount of time

My recommendation for those starting their quiet time is to spend half an hour each day, with the goal of graduating to one hour. At first the 30 minutes will seem like ages, but soon the time will fly by. You'll want to place more time in your schedule to seek the living God. The reason for setting a specific amount of time is to help you persevere through the dry spells. C. Peter Wagner writes ,"It is more advisable to start with quantity than quality in daily prayer time. First, program time. The quality will usually follow."[2]

---

2. Peter Wagner, *Prayer Shield* (Ventura, California: Regal, 1992), 86.

Try IT!

How do you feel about the idea of spending 30 minutes daily with the Lord?

_____

_____

_____

_____

_____

_____

_____

_____

_____

The key is not to give up. As in all relationships, the more time you spend with the person, the more comfortable you will feel. You'll understand the person better and enjoy each other more fully. As you consistently spend time with God, you'll notice a new freedom in His presence. The quantity of time will become more qualitative as you grow in your relationship with Him.

Do IT!
Commit yourself to spending 30 minutes daily with the Lord.
Make it your first priority.

Remember IT!

Summarize in your own words the main insight that you received from this lesson

_____

_____

_____

_____

_____

_____

_____

Main points:
1. Jesus invites us to spend time with Him at a specific time each day. For many, it's best to spend quality time with God in the morning; others prefer the evening or afternoon.
2. The key to determining when you will have your quiet time is discovering when you are most alert and can spend enough time.
3. Consistency is important in developing the daily habit of a quiet time.

Apply IT!

1. What have been your obstacles to a consistent, daily quiet time? (e.g., drowsiness etc.).
2. Decide on the exact time of your daily appointment with God. Then set your alarm or schedule in advance to make sure that you keep your commitment (if necessary to be awake, drink coffee, jog, etc.).
3. Decide on the amount of quiet time that best suits you.
4. Spend that amount of quiet time daily for the next two weeks.

Making Contact with God

Scientists have invested many millions of dollars trying to contact aliens from outer space. I'm referring to a research program called SETI (the search for extra terrestrial intelligence). These scientists assume that there must be an earth-like planet orbiting a star like our own somewhere among the billions of galaxies. SETI has now signed up over three million home computer users to analyze the radio telescope data that it sends out and receives from these distant stars.

No contact has ever been made. Silence. The aliens aren't talking.

The good news is that the God of the universe is talking! He sent His Son down to this earth to make contact with us. Then He gave us the Holy Spirit to live within those who believe. We can have constant contact through the Holy Spirit. And the God of the universe also gave us His divine book to guide us. God loves to keep in close contact with His children.

Where to meet with God

Noise is part of the modern world of traffic, computers, and cell phones. We have grown so accustomed to noise that we feel uncomfortable with silence.

Jesus ministered to the clamoring crowds, but He also needed to "close the door" in order to commune with the Father. The gospel of Luke tells us, "Jesus went out to a mountainside to pray, and spent the night praying to God. When morning came, he called his disciples to him and chose twelve of them" (6:12–13).

Just as Jesus left the noise of the multitude to seek the Father, I would urge you (as much as possible) to leave behind the noise of work, ministry and family in order to seek God. We can't expect to enter into the holy presence of God while sitting in front of the TV, being interrupted by telephone calls or driving in the car on the way to work.

The Greek word Jesus uses in Matthew 6:6 for "room" is tameon, which refers to the place in the Old Testament temple where the treasures were stored. When we enter into that special "room" and seek God in the quiet time, He reveals to us His riches and fills us with His Spirit.

Variety of secret places

Whether your "room" is your bedroom, the rooftop, a park or a vacant field, the important thing is the ability to "close the door" to the noise and cares of daily life.

Try IT!

Here are some possible secret places. Which ones do you like best?
□ Bedroom
□ Park
□ Office
□ Beach
□ Backyard
□ Forest
□ Garden
□ Garage
□ Bathroom
Why do you like the ones you chose?

_____

_____

_____

Even in the midst of a cluttered, hurried world, God provides us with many opportunities to seek Him. During one New York winter in 1984, I spent my daily quiet time in a bathroom. The only available seat was the toilet. The trick was having my devotions before my roommates woke up and needed to use the facilities! On normal occasions I spend my quiet time in my home office, but when possible I delight to seek God outdoors (e.g., forest, park or lake). The only criterion for determining your secret place is to make sure that quietness reigns supreme. What secret place do you find the most desirable? Where have you spent time with God in the past?

Try IT!

Potential distractions:
□ Ringing phone
□ Doorbell
□ Kids clamoring
□ Hunger pangs
□ Loud music
□ T.V.
□ Internet
What is your most common distraction?

_____

_____

_____

_____

Posture

God is a person who wants to communicate with us. He's not overly concerned with how we approach Him. He's mainly concerned that we do spend time in His presence. The Bible endorses a wide variety of postures.

Try IT!

Which posture do you normally use?

☐ Kneeling (Ezra 9:5)
☐ Falling on one's face (Exodus 4:31)
☐ Bending over (2 Kings 18:22)
☐ Bowing the head (Isaiah 58:5)
☐ Standing before the Lord (Nehemiah 9:2)
☐ Throwing oneself down (Deuteronomy 9:18)
☐ Lifting up hands (Psalm 63:4)

Why do you like a particular postture? (or perhaps you like a posture not mentioned on the list)

_____

_____

_____

_____

_____

Posture is pleasing to God only when it expresses the reality of the heart. To painfully prostrate yourself before God for hours during your quiet time only because you think you're supposed to, would displease God. God hates religious ritual that is not backed up by sincerity. Follow God's leading when choosing postures in your quiet time (kneeling, prostrating yourself, etc.).

Finding God

During the early years of European exploration of South America, a sailing ship ran out of drinking water near the mouth of the Amazon River. This river has the largest volume of fresh water of any river in the world. The sailors could not see land and thought they were in the middle of the ocean. Several died from thirst. Finally, in desperation, one sailor leaned over the side and drank, only to find that the ship had been sailing through fresh water for days. You are surrounded by the clean, fresh water of God's love and grace. It is all around you. Quiet time with God helps you to drink from His presence and quench your spiritual thirst.

Because God is everywhere at once, we don't need to meet with Him at one particular place or in one particular position. But we do need to meet with Him. The Bible often encourages us to seek after God.

Try IT!

Read Jeremiah 29:13–14a.
What is the promise in this Scripture?

_____

_____

_____

How do you plan on "finding God" in your devotional time?

_____

_____

_____

_____

_____

_____

_____

In the New Testament, there are many similar exhortations: "Without faith it is impossible to please God, because anyone who comes to him must believe that he exists and that he rewards those who earnestly seek him" (Hebrews 11:6).

God obviously wants us to exert effort to seek after Him and desire Him. He wants us to do this not in a weak, meager manner but with red-hot devotion. Passion. We play a part and God has His part. God will reveal Himself to the seeker. But we must seek.

When we seek God in our quiet time, He's pleased by our dependence on Him for every decision, concern and difficulty. When I'm struggling with family, finances or future, I've learned to go directly to Jesus. I've discovered that He longs to see me in that state of trust and dependence. Jim Cymbala, author of Fresh Wind, Fresh Fire, says, "I've discovered an astonishing truth: God is attracted to weakness. He can't resist those who humbly and honestly admit how desperately they need him. Our weakness, in fact, makes room for his power."[1]

Instead of coming to God with preconceived plans and agendas, seeking God helps us to look to Him only in utter dependence upon Him. We have nowhere else to turn but Jesus. Romans 8:26–27 says, "In the same way, the Spirit helps us in our weakness. We do not know what we ought to pray for, but the Spirit himself intercedes for us with groans that words cannot express. And he who searches our hearts knows the mind of the Spirit, because the Spirit intercedes for the saints in accordance with God's will."

Do IT!
During your quiet time, continue in the presence of the Lord until you feel His joy.

---

1. Jim Cymbala, Fresh Wind, Fresh Fire (Grand Rapids: Zondervan, 1997), 19.

Try IT!

Tips on Seeking God:
- ☐ Seek God Himself, rather than His reward.
- ☐ Persist in seeking Him even when you don't feel His presence.
- ☐ Expect to find Him and experience His joy.
- ☐ Refuse to allow your quiet time to become a sterile exercise.

Which of the following tips is the most helpful to you? Why?

_____

_____

_____

_____

_____

_____

_____

_____

_____

_____

God wants to reveal Himself

God desires us to seek Him because He longs to reveal Himself to us. God is not playing hide-and-seek with us, hoping that we don't find Him. He tells us, rather, that if we seek Him we will find Him. To find God simply means to experience His presence, to discover His will for our lives and to grow to know Him more intimately.

Try IT!

Read John 15:5.
What is Jesus saying here?

_____

_____

How can you apply this to your own life?

_____

_____

_____

_____

_____

_____

_____

_____

_____

_____

God isn't waiting for us to work ourselves into a frenzy trying to earn merit badges before He reveals Himself. God longs to reveal Himself. God delights in revealing Himself to the seeker—it's only a matter of time before He'll reveal Himself to you.

When we seek after God, we're actually saying: "God, I need You. Unless You come through, I have no hope."

Memorize IT!
Psalm 16:11: "You have made known to me the path of life; you will fill me with joy in your presence, with eternal pleasures at your right hand."

Discover His joy

God pours this joy into our lives and satisfies our deepest needs. If you'll concentrate on seeking God first, you will not only find God, but also receive the fruit of joy that is part of entering His presence.

Try IT!

Read Psalm 16:11.
What do we find in His presence?

_____

_____

Do you remember a time when you were joyful in Christ's presence? Describe it:

_____

_____

_____

_____

God Himself is our reward. God said to Abraham, "I am your shield, your very great reward" (Genesis 15:1). As you seek God diligently in your daily quiet time, not only will you find yourself growing in your intimacy with the Almighty, you will discover that knowing God is your greatest reward.

Remember IT!

Write out a prayer asking God to help you understand and apply one principle from this lesson.

_____

_____

_____

_____

_____

_____

Main points:
1. God desires that we pick a particular place for our quiet time where we can "close the door" to noise and outside activities.
2. God desires to reveal Himself to us, even though we will most likely experience spiritual dry spells. Yet, if we persevere, God is waiting for us at the end of that period.
3. God's joy is an indicator that we've actually found Him, but the best reward of seeking God is to find God Himself.

Apply IT!

1. Choose the physical location where you will spend time with God. Determine if that place enhances solitude and quietness. If not, choose another private place.
2. What are some of the hindrances you have experienced when seeking God?
3. Check the joy level in your heart after spending time in His presence. Do you sense that He has filled you?
4. Ask God to fill you with His joy in your quiet time.

Receiving from God

I really wanted to go astray, but I couldn't do it," Owen told us.

As Bible college students in Alberta, Canada, we were having our weekly testimony and encouragement time. Scrunched together at one end of a long, narrow dorm hall, we listened intently to Owen's testimony.

"As a teenager I tried drinking, smoking, and partying with non-Christians. The amazing thing is that every time I tried to sin, God's Word kept flooding my mind.

"As a child, my parents insisted that I memorize large portions of Scripture. When I wanted to rebel as a teenager, those Bible verses kept popping into my mind at the most inopportune moments. I tried listening to loud rock 'n' roll music to drown it out, yet in my silent moments, God's Word jumped out at me.

"I became upset at my parents for insisting that I memorize the Bible. Now, however, I thank God for them. As you can tell, God's Word won the battle, and here I am in Bible school."

Owen ended his testimony by reading Psalm 119:11: "I have hidden your word in my heart that I might not sin against you."

Reading God's Word

The Bible is God's love letter to us, instructing us on how to live a holy, successful life. It will not only keep you from sin, but it will reveal who God is.

You will begin to understand His nature, how much He loves you, and His perfect plan for your life. With God's Word filling your heart, you will then naturally flow into worship, confession of sin, listening to His voice and praying for others.

Go to the source

There are many great devotional guides on the market today. My only caution is that you don't allow any book or guide to replace God's Holy Word. These tools are only faint mirrors of the Bible.

The Bible is without error. This is not true of other books or guides. We can read the Bible with full confidence, knowing that everything written is worthy to be fully trusted (2 Timothy 3:16). As you open God's Word in the quiet time, you can be assured that God Himself is speaking to you.

Before reading the Bible, ask God for His wisdom. You might say, "Holy Spirit, help me understand the Bible and apply it to my daily life." This is a prayer that God loves to hear and answer.

Try IT!

True or false:
- ☐ The Bible can be trusted 100%.
- ☐ The Bible can only be understood by experts.
- ☐ The Bible helps us to know God more intimately.

Establish a Bible-reading plan

There are a lot of great Bible-reading plans. It is important to establish a systematic plan of Bible reading for your quiet time. I use the One-Year Bible (or at least the plan that the one-year Bible follows). The One-Year Bible has all the books of the Bible, arranged into daily readings that allow you to progress through the Bible in one year.

I highly recommend the One-Year Bible because it features a balanced diet that includes a daily portion from the Old Testament, New Testament, Psalms and Proverbs. And if you're faithful in its plan, you can rejoice on December 31 for having read the entire Bible!

Try IT!

Read Psalm 1:1–3.
How does David describe the person who meditates on God's Word continually?

_____

_____

_____

How are you going to apply these verses in your own life?

_____

_____

_____

_____

_____

For those who feel the pace of the One-Year Bible is too fast and would prefer to go more slowly through the Bible, another balanced diet would be to read an entire New Testament book (a chapter per day), then read an entire Old Testament book (a chapter per day). Supplement each day's reading with a Psalm or Proverb. One place to look for a Bible reading plan is: http://www.biblegateway.com/resources/reading plans.

Do IT!

Determine the Bible reading plan you will use.
Each day in your quiet time, read the portion of Scripture
your plan requires during your quiet time.

More than study

Your Bible-reading time should go beyond general Bible knowledge and lead to the application of God's truth to your life. Contemporary devotional author, Richard Foster, says, "A vast difference exists between the study of Scripture and the devotional reading of Scripture. In the study of Scripture a high priority is placed upon interpretation; what it means. In the devotional reading of Scripture a high priority is placed upon application: what it means for me."[2]

Meditating on God's Word

The dictionary defines meditation as the concentration of the mind on just one thing, in order to aid mental or spiritual development. It involves the act of thinking about something deeply and carefully. Words to describe meditation include consider, reflect and think.

Christian meditation, in contrast to Eastern meditation, contends that there is one true God who exists in three distinct persons: Father, Son and Holy Spirit. It assumes that people are sinful and need a Savior. God, the creator of this world, has given us a Bible free from error.

Unlike Eastern meditation, when we meditate on God's Word we don't place our minds in a passive state. Instead, we affirm that God's Word is truth and that God communicates to us directly through His Word. We actively seek to understand God's Word and how it applies to our lives. This results in increased understanding, a transformed life and God's blessing.

Meditation on the Scriptures is prayerful reflection with a view to understanding and application. The goal is to conform your life to God's will by prayerfully thinking about how to relate God's Word to your life

Joshua 1:8 says, "Do not let this Book of the Law depart from your mouth; meditate on it day and night, so that you may be careful to do everything written in it. Then you will be prosperous and successful." From this verse, what should be the source of your meditation? What

---

2. Richard Foster, *Celebration of Discipline* (New York: Harper & Row, 1978), 60.

is the relationship between meditation and application? What are the results of meditation?

Try IT!

Practice these steps to meditation:

1. Pray over a passage of Scripture.
2. Concentrate on it, perhaps repeating it again and again silently to yourself.

Meditation leads to memorization

Meditation of Scripture centers on internalizing and personalizing a passage. It's the process of thinking and rethinking over a passage of Scripture until you understand its meaning and application to your own life. The written word becomes God's Living Word. Memorization is the natural outcome of meditation. Once you know a verse or passage so intimately, you'll have it memorized; it will be part of you.

There are so many great benefits of memorizing Scripture. We're told that those who hide God's Word in their heart are able to resist temptation (Matthew 4:1–11), receive victory over sin (Psalm 119:11), and gain excellent understanding (Psalm 119:98–100).

Try IT!

Helps for memorization:

- Understand the thoughts behind the words rather than just the words. The goal is not just to memorize a verse(s), but to understand it and to apply it to your daily life.
- Realize that there is no such thing as a bad memory--only memories that haven't been trained. Anyone can develop his or her memory through continual discipline.
- Quote the verse out loud. This will help you to not only see the verse but also hear it.
- Memorize a Bible passage (several verses completing a whole thought) rather than one isolated verse. This will help you to better understand the context.
- Continually review the verse(s).

Listening to God's voice

Our tendency is to want someone else to speak to God on our behalf and just tell us plainly what He wants. The children of Israel were fearful of going directly to God but said to Moses, "Speak to us yourself and we will listen. But do not have God speak to us or we will die" (Exodus 20:18).

God speaks in the silence

The Bible tells about a boy prophet named Samuel who God awoke in the middle of the night to whisper truth about the future of Israel: "... Samuel was lying down in the temple of the LORD, where the ark of God was. Then the LORD called Samuel. Samuel answered, "Here I am" (1 Samuel 3:3–4). In the deep stillness, when the lights had gone out, God revealed Himself to Samuel.

Try IT!

True or false:

☐ God only speaks when we're in church.

☐ God speaks anywhere and everywhere.

☐ God prefers to speak through preachers on Sunday morning .

God can speak anytime, anywhere, and anyplace. He's not bound to speak in a temple or in a physical place. The most common time, however, for God to speak is when His children are spending quality time in His presence. During quiet time, God has our attention. We've dedicated time to Him. Our hearts are prepared through the Word, worship and confession. The static is gone. The signal comes in loud and clear. We're tuned into the right station. God will most frequently speak to us when we are quiet and in His presence.

Memorize IT!
Psalm 119:11: "I have hidden your word in my heart that I might not sin against you."

His sheep know His voice

In John 10:10 Jesus talks about sheep following the good shepherd: "He calls his own sheep by name and leads them out ... and his sheep follow him because they know his voice. But they will never follow a stranger; in fact, they will run away from him because they do not recognize a stranger's voice" (vs. 3–5). Jesus, the good shepherd, desires to guide us through each step of the way. He impresses upon us His will and direction.

God's voice	Satan's voice
● Accompanied with peace	● Accompanied with fear
● Gentle wisdom	● Confusion
● Freedom	● Pressure
● Power to accomplish the task	● Guilt because of difficulty of task

The word "impression" best describes how God normally speaks to people. He impresses on our mind and spirit His will and desires. And God's impression will never contradict the Bible. As I've spent time in His presence, I've become familiar with His gentle nudges in my own life. I'm not sure how to describe these gentle nudges, except to say that they are peaceful, gentle, and easy to understand and apply. My inward reaction to these impressions is "Yes, that's it." These impressions might show me who I should call, where I should go, or what I should do.

Try IT!

How do you know when God has spoken to you?

_____

_____

_____

Remember IT!

What had the most impact on you in this lesson?

_____

_____

_____

_____

_____

_____

Main points:
1. The application of the Word of God takes precedence over observation and interpretation.
2. It's best to have a daily Bible-reading plan. The author recommends the One-Year Bible.
3. Memorization is the result of deep meditation.
4. God desires to speak to us directly, and he normally speaks to us in the silence of our quiet time.

Apply IT!

1. Decide on a particular Bible-reading goal (read the entire Bible in one year, two years, etc.).
2. Reflect on Joshua 1:7–8 and Psalm 1. Allow these verses to penetrate deeply into your own life. Ask yourself what changes you need to make in your life as a result of these verses.
3. Take one or two Bible verses from your daily Bible reading and meditate upon them. Then memorize those same verses.
4. Do you remember a time when God spoke to you? What did He say?
5. Wait in stillness before God and seek to hear His impressions upon your heart.

Entering God's Presence

"And David sat before the Lord" (1 Chronicles 17:16). This phrase is one of the best examples of pure worship in the Bible. God had just reminded David of his lowly background as a shepherd of sheep, and of how He had raised him up as king over all Israel. God had reiterated all that He had done for David in the past.

And not only had God pledged to continue to bless David in the present, He also promised to bless and prosper David's future offspring as well: "I declare to you that the LORD will build a house for you: When your days are over and you go to be with your fathers, I will raise up your offspring to succeed you, one of your own sons, and I will establish his kingdom" (1 Chronicles 17:10–11).

Hearing these words, David lacked the strength to stand. He simply sat in a heap of gratitude. Words were meaningless. Time stood still. Finally, David responds with a grateful heart:

Who am I, O LORD God, and what is my family, that you have brought me this far? And as if this were not enough in your sight, O God, you have spoken about the future of the house of your servant. You have looked on me as though I were the most exalted of men, O LORD God. What more can David say to you for honoring your servant? For you know your servant, O LORD. For the sake of your servant and according to your will, you have done this great thing and made known all these great promises (1 Chronicles 17:16–17).

Worshiping God

Worship is a natural response to a grateful heart. It's simply acknowledging who God is and what He's done. Worship is the result. Some people think that worship is only a Sunday morning event. In reality, there's no better place to express that gratefulness than in your quiet time. Why? Because worship in quiet time is all about Him. You don't have to worry about your performance or trying to impress God or others—just be yourself. He looks into your heart. He sees your nakedness and brokenness and accepts you anyway. Sit before the Lord and thank Him.

Try IT!

How does worship impact your relationship with God?

_____

_____

_____

Describe the worship experience you're having now in your quiet time?

_____

_____

_____

_____

_____

_____

_____

_____

The meaning of worship

The Old Testament word for worship literally means to prostrate oneself on the ground—absolute humility before the Creator. Most of the words that refer to worshiping God are used in physical terms: lying prostrate on one's face, kneeling, standing, clapping, lifting up the arms, dancing, lifting the head and bowing the head.

In the New Testament, the meaning of the word worship is even more intimate. It literally means, "to kiss." Worship under the new covenant is a very intimate experience of submission to the living God. It's drawing close to a living God who longs to have a close relationship with us. It's spending intimate time in His presence in order to get to know Him. And then throughout eternity we'll be worshiping God. The book of Revelation has many vivid descriptions of what we'll be doing throughout all eternity. Revelation 4:8–11, for example, describes what goes on in heaven:

Day and night they never stop saying: "Holy, holy, holy is the Lord God Almighty, who was, and is, and is to come." Whenever the living creatures give glory, honor and thanks to him who sits on the throne and who lives forever and ever, the twenty-four elders fall down before him who sits on the throne, and worship him who lives for ever and ever. They lay their crowns before the throne and say: "You are worthy, our Lord and God, to receive glory and honor and power, for you created all things, and by your will they were created and have their being.

Since we'll be worshiping God throughout eternity, how can we become more passionate about worship now?

Try IT!

True or false:

☐ Worship is the natural response of a grateful heart to God's grace, mercy, and love.

☐ Worship can happen anytime and in any place.

☐ God prefers worship in a building on Sunday.

Worship in the quiet time

To worship in the quiet time, you might sing a hymn or favorite worship chorus, wait in silence, or read a psalm. Many people allow praise and worship to flow naturally from Bible reading and meditation. Paul Cedar writes, "Sometimes a certain song or hymn of praise will come to mind when I am meditating on my Bible reading or when I am reading one of the psalms as an expression of praise and worship to God. Otherwise, I proceed sequentially through my hymns and praise songs."[3]

Try IT!

Read Revelation 4:8–12.
How would you describe what is taking place in heaven, according to these verses?

_____

_____

_____

Why should we be stirred to worship continually here on earth in light of what's taking place throughout eternity?

_____

_____

_____

_____

_____

_____

---

3. Paul Cedar, *A Life of Prayer* (Nashville: Word, 1998), 191.

Worship in quiet time is a heart issue. Never allow worship to decline to mere duty. Don't let the awe and wonder of God be choked out by canned performances or repetition of words you don't really mean. Get to the heart of worship. It's all about Jesus.

Memorize IT!
Psalm 95:6: "Come, let us bow down in worship, let us kneel before the LORD our Maker."

Confession

I remember when God revealed to me that I was harboring unforgiveness toward a particular pastor. Two days earlier, this pastor had offended me, and I felt that I had every right to be upset by his action. Unfortunately, I failed to see that my own bitterness had stripped me of joy. I felt a pressure and slight depression when going to bed after this incident, but I didn't know why. The next morning, God spoke clearly to me. I needed to confess my sin of bitterness. After confessing my bitterness and rebellion, the heaviness lifted and I felt a new freedom.

Try IT!
Why is it so important to make confession of sin a regular habit?

_____

_____

_____

_____

_____

_____

Our constant prayer in quiet time should be this prayer of David: "Search me, O God, and know my heart; test me and know my anxious thoughts. See if there is any offensive way in me, and lead me in the way everlasting" (Psalm 139:23–24). Only God can reveal sin's deceitfulness. We cannot.

Unhindered communion

Many churches use spiritual retreats to help members grow in holiness and receive healing from sinful, satanic bondages. When I attended my first Encounter Retreat, God worked powerfully as I confessed bitterness and anger, as well as other sins. God transformed my life, and I experienced an incredible new freedom and liberty.

Yet, as the months passed, I noticed that I still struggled in some of those areas. I realized that in order to remain free, I needed to approach God on a daily basis, confessing any reoccurring sin. God showed me that I needed the strength of my daily quiet time to walk in freedom.

Camps and retreats are great. God uses them to speak to us clearly and powerfully. But there's a danger in living today on yesterday's one-time experience. We need to walk with God on a daily basis. 1 John 1:8–10 says, "If we claim to be without sin, we deceive ourselves and the truth is not in us. If we confess our sins, he is faithful and just and will forgive us our sins and purify us from all unrighteousness. If we claim we have not sinned, we make him out to be a liar and his word has no place in our lives."

Stay cleansed

In biblical times, dirt roads were the norm. Since everyone wore sandals, no matter how hard a person tried to keep his feet clean, they would naturally pick up the dirt and dust of the Roman roads. Foot washing wasn't a religious rite; it was a practical necessity.

Even as mature Christians, we unconsciously pick up bad habits and wrong thoughts. The world, flesh and the devil lurk in the most unexpected places. You can hardly watch TV, listen to the radio, drive down the freeway or overhear a conversation without seeing or hearing ungodly conduct.

Do IT!

Take time now and pray through these steps to see if there is any area of your life where God wants to set you free.

1. *Ask God to reveal hidden areas of sin in your life.*
2. *Acknowledge your sin before God.*
3. *Confess your sin.*
4. *Experience God's cleansing and renewal.*

Remember IT!

What had the most impact on you in this lesson?

_____

_____

_____

_____

_____

_____

Main points:

1. In the Old Testament the word for worship meant to prostrate oneself before God; The New Testament word for worship literally means, "to kiss."
2. Worship in quiet time is the act of expressing our praise, thanks and adoration to the One we love.
3. Daily confession is the way to maintain communion and fellowship with God.

Apply IT!

1. Look for the passages on worship in the book of Revelation. Meditate upon them.
2. Read a psalm in your quiet time, expressing your worship directly to God.
3. Ask God to reveal areas of sin in your life. Confess the sin(s) that God reveals.

Praying to God

'll never forget that Monday morning in Seoul, Korea in April 1997 when I took a bus to Prayer Mountain, a former cemetery converted into a mountain of prayer. An estimated 10,000 people pass through this prayer mountain every week. The Yoido Full Gospel Church has carved hundreds of caves into the side of this mountain for the purpose of prayer. It was exciting to walk by the prayer caves and hear the cries of God's people ascending to His throne.

These Korean believers reminded me of Epaphras, a person who Paul said, "is always wrestling in prayer for you, that you may stand firm in all the will of God, mature and fully assured" (Colossians 4:12). The verb "wrestle" in this verse literally means to fight or struggle.

I need to wrestle more in prayer, I said to myself. *I lack fervency in prayer.* Compared to the Korean Christians, my prayer life was halfhearted. I left Korea inspired to strengthen the fervency of my prayer life.

In your quiet time, pray with fervency and earnestness. Persist in your prayers for your unsaved parents, a lost office worker or rebellious children—knowing that God is willing to answer your prayers. As you pray according to His will, God will answer your prayers, and you will gain confidence in approaching God in the quiet time.

Prayer

Webster's dictionary defines prayer first as an act of communion with God and second as reverent petition made to God. Prayer is an intimate dialogue between Father and child. Petition, while important, is a result of our communion with Him.

In its purest sense, prayer is simply communicating with God. The Bible does tell us, however, that effective prayer follows certain guidelines and requirements (e.g., praying according to His will, asking in Jesus Name, etc.).

To understand how to pray, we must study God's Word. Thus, the study of God's Word is the first discipline of the quiet time. In my own quiet time, I like to receive understanding and spiritual strength from the Word and worship before prayer. As I understand God's will through the Word, I'm more encouraged to commune with God and pray for others. Allowing God to speak to us first will influence what we choose to say to Him—what we consider to be most relevant and important.

God's willingness to answer

A particular son asked his father for the inheritance money, which he wanted to spend on his own pleasures. His own recklessness caused him to lose the money rather than spend it wisely. In a state of misery, living with the pigs, he decided to go back to his father and beg for mercy. The son was sure that his father would reject him. He was trying to figure out what to say, but his father only wanted to pour out his love, care, and blessing. The father wanted to do far more than his son could ask or imagine.

God has plans to bless us far more than you or I could imagine. While we're sleeping, the heavenly Father is planning wonderful things that will culminate in a heavenly dwelling that we can't even begin to understand right now. The Psalmist says that the Heavenly Father's thoughts towards us are more than the sand by the seashore (Psalm 139:17–18).

Try IT!

Read Ephesians 3:20.
What does this say about God's ability to answer our prayer requests?

_____

_____

_____

What are you asking God to do in your life at this time? Do you believe God will answer?

_____

_____

_____

_____

_____

_____

_____

God encourages us to pray by revealing His intention to answer. The first guideline for effective prayer is the knowledge that God desires to respond. God not only hears our prayers but He also plans to answer. And because of what Jesus Christ has done for us, we can approach the throne of grace with confidence, knowing that our prayers will be heard and answered according to His plan (Hebrews 4:12).

Jesus revealed throughout the gospels how much the Father desires to answer prayer:

- And I will do whatever you ask in my name, so that the Son may bring glory to the Father. You may ask me for anything in my name, and I will do it (John 14:13–14).
- If you remain in me and my words remain in you, ask whatever you wish, and it will be given you (John 15:7).
- In that day you will no longer ask me anything. I tell you the truth, my Father will give you whatever you ask in my name. Until now you have not asked for anything in my name. Ask and you will receive, and your joy will be complete (John 16:23–24).
- Jesus says, "If you, then, though you are evil, know how to give good gifts to your children, how much more will your Father in heaven give good gifts to those who ask him!" (Matthew 7:11).

Praying according to the will of God

Most believers need a jolt of confidence to continue praying. The apostle John wrote precisely to this group when he said, "This is the confidence we have in approaching God: that if we ask anything according to his will, he hears us. And if we know that he hears us— whatever we ask—we know that we have what we asked of him" (1 John 5:14–15). This means that not all requests are according to God's will. One key reason for reading and mediating on the Bible in the quiet time is to make sure our will is one with His. Often we'll simply say, "May Your will be done." Or we might sense He's leading us to fervently pray in a particular direction. When we believe we're praying according to the will of God, doubt vanishes.

Try IT!

Read Matthew 6:10.
What should guide our prayers according this verse?

_____

_____

How do you know that you're praying according to God's will?

_____

_____

_____

_____

_____

_____

_____

_____

Praying according to the will of God is the only known remedy for doubt. When you know you are praying according to the will of God, you will be motivated to continue, knowing that God will grant your request.

When determining the will of God, the first place to look is the Bible. This is where the quiet time comes in. Studying and meditating on the Word of God injects confidence into weary believers. We can be confident that God wills what His Word has already declared.

Spending time in God's presence will help you discern God's specific leading. As you study the Word, meditate on His promises, worship in His presence, and listen to His voice, He will show you His specific plan for your life.

Try IT!

Read Matthew 7:21.
Do you believe God has an individual plan for you?

_____

_____

How do you primarily determine God's will for your life?

_____

_____

_____

_____

_____

_____

_____

Intercession

Even though God desires to answer prayer, He does expect us to persist in prayer. Intercessory prayer is an earnest request to God on behalf of another. Unlike the wicked judge in Luke 19, our heavenly judge is our heavenly Father. He loves us and cares for us. He wants us to bring our petitions to Him; He promises to respond quickly. Luke says this about our Heavenly Father: "And will not God bring about justice for his chosen ones, who cry out to him day and night?

Will he keep putting them off? I tell you, he will see that they get justice, and quickly" (Luke 18: 7–8).

Do IT!

Think of a good friend that needs Jesus. Begin praying for that person's salvation each day, believing that the Holy Spirit will work in that person's life.

Prayer in quiet time is not only designed to edify us and meet our own needs. God wants us to enter the battleground and pray fervently for others. Just remember that intercession is hard work and requires persistence. In your quiet time, you will probably pray for certain individuals on a daily basis—your unsaved dad, sister, cousin or fellow worker. There are other items you might pray for on a weekly basis. It's helpful to make a list of those things you'll pray for each day of the week. Then record the answers as God responds. Scripture gives many examples of intercession:

- Job interceded for his companions, and the Lord made him prosperous again (Job 42:10).
- Abraham interceded for his nephew Lot, who was living in Sodom. He asked God to spare his nephew and be merciful toward him (Genesis 18:16–33).
- Moses interceded for God's people, who were facing God's judgment. Moses pleaded with God to act in mercy rather than judgment (Exodus 32:9–14).
- Samuel recognized his duty to pray for God's people. He even considered it a sin not to do so. He said, "As for me, far be it from me that I should sin against the LORD by failing to pray for you" (1 Samuel 12:23).
- Jesus Christ interceded for his disciples: "I pray for them. I am not praying for the world, but for those you have given me, for they are yours. ... Holy Father, protect them by the power of your name—the name you gave me—so that they may be one as we are one" (John 17:9, 11).

Try IT!

Jot down names of people who need your regular intercessory prayers:

_____

_____

_____

_____

_____

_____

Begin to pray for these people in your quiet time.

Don't give up

Your prayers can and will make a difference. Jesus said in the Lord's Prayer, "your will be done on earth as it is in heaven" (Matthew 6:10). Asking for God's will to be done is the fuel for intercessory prayer. Pray that God will accomplish His will on earth as it is in heaven.

George Mueller prayed throughout his lifetime for five friends to know Jesus Christ. The first one came to Christ after five years. Within ten years, two more of them received Christ. Mueller prayed constantly for over twenty-five years, and the fourth man was finally saved. For his fifth friend, he prayed until the time of his death, and this friend, too, came to Christ a few months after Mueller died. For this last friend, Mueller had prayed for almost fifty-two years.

Memorize IT!
Colossians 4:2: "Devote yourselves to prayer, being watchful and thankful."

Remember IT!

What is one thing from this lesson you want to share with someone close to you?

_____

_____

_____

_____

_____

_____

Main points:
1. God works through prayer to transform us, so that we might pray according to His will.
2. We can pray with confidence when we know that we're praying according to God's will.
3. Intercession is praying to God on behalf of someone else.

Apply IT!

1. Find a Bible verse(s) to support a particular prayer request. This will help you pray with more fervency and confidence, knowing you're praying according to God's will.
2. As you pray for God to work in your own life (e.g., freedom from bitterness, more joyfulness), record those changes in a journal.
3. Write down on a list the names of those for whom you want to intercede.

Growing in Spiritual Power

J onathan Edwards (1703–1758), a famous New England preacher, played a pivotal role in the spiritual revival called the Second Great Awakening. Before he preached one of his famous sermons that helped initiate the revival, he had fasted and prayed for three days, while saying over and over again, "Give me, New England! Give me New England!" When he got up off his knees and made his way to the pulpit, they say that he looked as if he had been gazing straight into the face of God. Before he opened his lips to speak, the Spirit's conviction fell upon his audience.

What allows a person to grow in spiritual power and authority? One way is to draw close to God through fasting. Fasting and quiet time are not necessarily linked together. You are not going to fast every day in your quiet time. Yet because the goal of quiet time is to know God, and the main purpose of fasting is to enhance your spiritual sensitivity to God, on occasion you will want to supercharge your quiet time through the discipline of fasting.

Fasting

One of the key motivations for fasting (abstention from all or certain types of food) is that self-denial draws us closer to God. Fasting helps us to concentrate on God, pray more fervently and overcome personal bondages. Fasting helps us to hear God's voice because we become more sensitive to Him. It clears up the cobwebs in our brain and helps us see with spiritual eyes.

In Scripture we see several purposes for fasting: the discipline of self-control, dependence on God alone, and focusing on Him when seeking His guidance and help.

Try IT!

Reflect on Biblical reasons for fasting:

- To receive God's illumination and wisdom (Daniel 9:2, 3, 21, 22; 10:1-14)
- To overcome sin (Isaiah 58:6)
- To declare that God is the priority of our lives (Matthew 4:4)
- To increase personal holiness (Psalm 69:10)
- To have victory over Satan (Mark 9:29)

Can you think of other examples?

_____

_____

_____

_____

_____

In simple terms, fasting is avoiding eating all or certain types of food for the purpose of concentrating on God. Fasting is a way to focus on God alone when seeking His guidance and help. Fasting demonstrates your sincerity. Fasting helps believers become more sensitive to God's presence and hear His voice more clearly.

One reason for fasting is to petition God on behalf of someone else. When Haman influenced King Xerxes to sign a decree to destroy the Jews in the land, Mordecai asked Esther to intercede on the Jews' behalf. Esther replied to Mordecai:

Go, gather together all the Jews who are in Susa, and fast for me. Do not eat or drink for three days, night or day. I and my maids will fast as you do. When this is done, I will go to the king, even though it is against the law. And if I perish, I perish (Esther 4:16).

We know that God heard the cries of Esther and the Jews. He responded in a miraculous way.

Another great benefit of fasting is receiving God's direction. Often we fast because we need guidance. The apostles waited before the Lord in prayer and fasting until the Holy Spirit said, "Set apart for me Barnabas and Saul for the work to which I have called them" (Acts 13:2). When we fast and pray, we become more sensitive to God's leading.

Try IT!

Read Acts 14:23.
How did Paul and Barnabas appoint the elders?

_____

_____

_____

How does fasting increase prayer's effectiveness?

_____

_____

_____

_____

_____

_____

_____

_____

> **Do IT!**
> *Skip two meals (e.g., breakfast and lunch) and spend extra time in prayer and worship.*

The ABC's of fasting

Although there are various kinds of fasts, the most common one is to abstain from food, but not drink, for a given period of time. Most people drink water while fasting, but some people drink coffee, tea and fruit juices. Here is a more complete listing of Bible fasts:

Complete fast	Normal fast	Partial fast	Group Fast
• Abstinence from eating food and drinking liquids • Example of Moses (Deut. 9:9; Exodus 34:28) • Other examples: Esther 4:16; Acts 9:9)	• Abstinence from all food and liquid with the exception of drinking water • Example of Jesus in the desert (Matthew 4:1–4).	• A restricted diet rather than a complete abstinence from food • Example of Daniel's partial fast (Daniel 9:3; 10:3)	• Fasting in a group setting. • Other examples: Joel 1:14; 2:15; Esther 4:16)

Be careful of your appearance when fasting. Jesus talks about this when he said, "When you fast, do not look somber as the hypocrites do, for they disfigure their faces to show men they are fasting. I tell you the truth, they have received their reward in full. But when you fast, put oil on your head and wash your face, so that it will not be obvious to men that you are fasting, but only to your Father, who is unseen; and your Father, who sees what is done in secret, will reward you" (Matthew 6:16–18).

The filling of the Spirit

Back in the 80s and 90s, most people used cassettes to record messages. I used my tape recorder a lot. Because batteries were expensive, I bought rechargeable ones that could be used over and over.

I could always tell when I needed to recharge them. The voice on the tape began to slow down ever so slightly until I couldn't recognize the person or the message. After the batteries were recharged and put back into the tape player, you could once again hear the voices on the tape perfectly.

Our own lives are similar. We run down. We need to be recharged daily with the filling of the Spirit. This recharging takes place in our quiet time. Afterwards, we can hear the voice of God and receive His direction more clearly. Without this daily filling, it's far more difficult to hear His voice and receive His direction.

Refreshed with living water

Jesus said, "If anyone is thirsty, let him come to me and drink. Whoever believes in me, as the Scripture has said, streams of living water will flow from within him. By this he meant the Spirit, whom those who believed in him were later to receive" (John 7:37–39).

Try IT!

Reread John 7:37–39.
Who can receive this living water?

_____

_____

_____

_____

_____

The ideal time to receive this living water is in our daily quiet time. During this time we are able to enter into communion with our heavenly Father, confessing known sins and listening to His voice. It's also a great time to ask Jesus to fill us with His Holy Spirit. With such a clear invitation from Jesus Christ Himself, there is no reason to be thirsty in the Christian life. If we come daily, asking Him to fill us with the Holy Spirit, our souls will be satisfied, and we will be equipped to face the dry desert around us.

God asks us to take two simple steps to be filled with the Spirit. First, we must confess all known sin. David says, If I had cherished sin in my heart, the Lord would not have listened" (Psalm 66:18). Second, ask the Holy Spirit to fill you. Jesus says, "Ask and it will be given to you; seek and you will find; knock and the door will be opened to you" (Matthew 7:7).

A continual filling

Paul tells us in Ephesians 5:18, "Do not get drunk on wine, which leads to debauchery [immoral behavior]. Instead, be filled with the Spirit." In the original Greek, the phrase "be filled" as found here is a present tense verb. Paul could have used the past tense or a future verb tense to signify a one-time filling; instead, he chose the present tense to denote that the filling of the Holy Spirit is not a one-time event but a continual experience.

Memorize IT!
Luke 11:13: "If you then, though you are evil, know how to give good gifts to your children, how much more will your Father in heaven give the Holy Spirit to those who ask him!"

It's all about control

Paul compares filling of the Spirit with drunkenness. The comparison between alcohol and the Spirit of God has everything to do with control. Many people drink alcohol because it causes them to lose themselves in a state of happiness and ecstasy. They feel that the alcohol makes words flow more easily and relations easier to develop.

The Holy Spirit also controls. The difference between the two is not the activity but the essence. Alcohol is an ingredient, a substance, a thing. The Holy Spirit, in contrast, is a person. The Holy Spirit is God, the third person of the Trinity. And as a person He wants to control us, if we'll let Him. While alcohol's control weakens us, the Spirit's control strengthens us.

Quiet time is the right atmosphere for the Holy Spirit to control our lives. When we seek His face, prepare our hearts, and ask Him to take over, He will respond.

D. L. Moody, the famous preacher of the nineteenth century, was scheduled to conduct a crusade in a particular city. At one minister's meeting a young man got up and asked, "Why do we have to have D. L. Moody anyway? After all, does he have a monopoly on the Holy Spirit?" After a quiet pause a saintly pastor rose to his feet and replied, "Young man, Mr. Moody may not have a monopoly on the Holy Spirit, but those of us who know him recognize that the Holy Spirit has a monopoly on him."

God is looking for men and women who desire above all else to be controlled by the Holy Spirit. Like D. L. Moody, the Holy Spirit wants to have a monopoly on you.

Remember IT!

What truth from this lesson impacted you the most?

_____

_____

_____

_____

_____

_____

_____

Main points:
1. The essence of fasting is to abstain from food in order to be more sensitive to God and His direction.
2. God wants to refresh us with His living water in our quiet time.

Apply IT!

1. Skip one meal
2. Skim through the book of Revelation, noticing all the verses that talk about angels, people, or creatures worshiping in heaven. Meditate upon them.
3. Read a psalm in your quiet time, expressing your worship directly to God.

Resting and Reflecting

The movie Chariots of Fire tells the story of British runners, Harold Abrahams and Eric Liddell, who won gold medals in the 100 and 400 meters. Liddell, who refused to race on Sunday, was forced to withdraw from his best event, the 100 meters. He entered the 400 meters instead and won.

While I agree that Sunday is an important day for Christians to celebrate because of Christ's resurrection, I also realize that most ministers work the hardest on that day and get the least amount of rest.

It's my conviction that more important than honoring one particular day of the week is the need to have one full day to rest and focus on God. Taking a full day of rest combined with a daily quiet time will help you grow spiritually and keep you refreshed for the rest of the week.

Taking a 24-hour "Sabbath" rest

God tells us that He made the Sabbath for us. God gave this principle to his people. Genesis 2:2 says, "By the seventh day God had finished the work he had been doing; so on the seventh day he rested from all his work. And God blessed the seventh day and made it holy, because on it he rested from all the work of creating that he had done." Though we are not under an Old Testament law that requires us to rest on a certain day, like Saturday, the principle of a 24-hour day of rest still applies today.

God wants us to rest once a week for 24 hours for our own health and happiness. He knows it's for our own good. Our bodies can only handle so much work. Taking a day off helps us concentrate on what God has done and helps renews our minds to focus on Him.

Try IT!

What is your number one obstacle for taking a 24-hour day of rest each week?

_____

_____

_____

_____

_____

_____

_____

Taking one day out of your calendar to rest will bring life balance to you and to all you do. You'll find yourself refreshed to face the challenges for the rest of the week. God has made our bodies to work very hard for six days per week. We read in Genesis that on the seventh day God had finished the work he had been doing; so on the seventh day he rested from all his work. And God blessed the seventh day and made it holy, because on it he rested from all the work of creating that he had done.

I'm convinced of the principle of taking one day off. It doesn't matter what day you take off—just do it! Currently it works for me and my family to take our day off on Saturday. Yet we've also used Friday as our day off in the past. The key is to discover what works best for you.

Try IT!

Read Leviticus 23:32.
What are God's people to do on their rest day?

_____

_____

_____

What are your workaholic tendencies?

_____

_____

_____

_____

_____

_____

_____

_____

During my day off, I focus on only doing those things that bring rest and relaxation. I don't look at my email, for example, because I might hear about urgent news that will bring worry rather than relaxation. I avoid personal "Joel Comiskey" work of any kind, although I gladly do normal family responsibilities during that time period (e.g., take our trash, wash dishes, etc.). Don't be a legalist. Don't condemn yourself when you have to perform particular chores on that day (e.g., dishes, a bathroom pipe breaks, etc.).

As a family we do something special together (e.g., go somewhere, watch a video, etc.). We always eat out, so my wife doesn't have to prepare a meal. We go to bed early and wake up late. I try to avoid caffeine on that day, so I can rest more fully. The key is rest.

I've inevitably found that I get my best work done immediately after my day off. My mind and body are refreshed. Taking a day off also helps me to work hard the entire week, knowing that on one day I will rest deeply. My body looks forward to it and intuitively knows when that day rolls around.

Do IT!
Take one 24-hour period of complete rest each week.
Make it a habit for the rest of your life.

Finding the rhythm

Try to take the same day off consistently each week. This will help you to get in a seven-day rhythm. Your body and soul will get into the habit of ceasing labor on that particular day. You'll find yourself working harder throughout the week, knowing that your day off is coming.

As mentioned earlier, cease from what you consider "work" for 24 hours. The main point is that you do things that you consider restful. Each person will have a different criterion for restful behavior.

Find out what is restful for you and what you consider "work." Refuse to worry about the stresses of life on that day. Meditate on God's goodness and love. I make it a point for that 24-hour period NOT to worry about anything. If I'm facing a major decision or worry, I make it a point not to dwell on it during that time period. I make Philippians 4:6–8 my theme verses during my day off:

Do not be anxious about anything, but in everything, by prayer and petition, with thanksgiving, present your requests to God. And the peace of God, which transcends all understanding, will guard your hearts and your minds in Christ Jesus. Finally, brothers, whatever is true, whatever is noble, whatever is right, whatever is pure, whatever is lovely, whatever is admirable—if anything is excellent or praiseworthy—think about such things.

Make sure you include God in your agenda. It's a great idea to go on a family outing or other restful activity. Just make sure that God plays a key role on the agenda during the day off (e.g., don't skip out on private and family devotions).

Try IT!

Read Matthew 11: 28–30.
According to these verses, what is God's desire for His children?

_____

_____

_____

Is your lifestyle burdensome or light/easy? How can a day off help?

_____

_____

_____

_____

_____

_____

> **Memorize IT!**
> **Hebrews 4:13: "Nothing in all creation is hidden from God's sight. Everything is uncovered and laid bare before the eyes of him to whom we must give account."**

Journaling

Journaling is writing down our thoughts, illuminations from God, application of Biblical truth, praise reports, accounts of struggles and whatever else we feel is important to write down. I find the practice of journaling an excellent way to rest and relieve anxiety. The process of journaling is therapeutic and restful. Here's an entry from one of my journals on February 8, 1997:

> What a struggle today. I was having a great devotion and really seeking Jesus. Suddenly the phone rang. _____was on the phone, and he just wanted to talk. Fifty minutes later, troubled, frustrated, etc. I hung up the phone. I didn't feel listened to, I didn't feel like I truly had a conversation, and yet worse, I tried to use the time to exhort him to treat _____better and he seemed to resist my effort.

Just a normal entry, but it shows how journaling can be a great way to untangle thoughts and express fears and frustrations to God.

During my quiet time, I often open my diary (journal) and look at pages of past entries. As I'm reading, I will remember the past situation—the conflict, the victory or the longing. I often find myself thinking, "Wow, time has passed so quickly. I'm so grateful for God's work in my life. He's never let me down."

Soon, your diary will become a refuge. You'll find yourself writing during times of pain, difficulty, confusion or joy. After a period of time elapses, this written record will become a source of encouragement as the promises of God are verified or as struggles finally end. You'll love to look back at what God has accomplished in your life.

I write in my diary for a variety of reasons: insight, victory, defeat, lessons learned, to list a few. My only rule is an internal one: I write when I feel the need to do so. I have no other formula. I don't try to write a lot or a little—just whenever I feel the need. Over the years,

I've discovered that I normally tend to journal when passing through a deep trial or period of confusion about God's will in my own life.

Try IT!

Do you keep a journal? Why or why not?

_____

_____

_____

_____

_____

_____

_____

_____

_____

_____

Reasons for a journal

One of the reasons to journal is to find comfort in times of trial. When everything is positive and normal, I don't feel the need to write. It is during times of conflict or defeat, or when I'm on the ground looking up, that my diary offers comfort.

Another reason is to clarify our own thinking. Writing down our thoughts helps us to see things from more than one perspective. Vague impressions or unclear thoughts begin to untangle themselves as we write them down. In some cases, we realize that we have knowledge we didn't know we possessed.

Finally, journaling helps us reflect back on what God has done in our lives. It's wonderful to look back and see how God has provided and guided our lives. Looking back on God's faithfulness gives us more confidence to face the future.

Try IT!

Times to review your journal
- Randomly during the quiet time
- Approximately every seven days
- Yearly as you review what God has done during the year

When do you find it best to review your journal? Why?

_____

_____

_____

_____

_____

_____

_____

Journaling tips

Maintain secrecy and privacy. You won't write with the same intensity unless you know that what you write is yours and yours alone. Your diary is between you and the living God. He sees what you've written: your hurts, fears, tears and groaning. The exercise of writing is to deepen your transparency before the Almighty.

Direct your thoughts to God. Your diary should be written to God. This doesn't mean you have to use God's name on every page; just remember that you are recording your thoughts, feelings, fears, hopes, prayer requests, and answers from God.

Just do it. Someone has said that a journey of a thousand miles begins with a single step. Start journaling now and make improvements as you go. You'll look back at your journal in the future and rejoice in what God has done in your life. You'll be able to reflect on His ongoing faithfulness and grace.

My book, *An Appointment with the King,* covers the topic of journaling in more detail (as well as all other aspects of the quiet time). You can buy it at www.joelcomiskeygroup.com or by calling 1-888-344-CELL.

Remember IT!

What stood out to you in this lesson?

_____

_____

_____

_____

_____

_____

Main points:
1. The Sabbath should not be a legalistic undertaking but one that brings freedom.
2. The purpose of the Sabbath is freedom: rest, relationship, and growth.
3. Writing your thoughts down on paper clarifies your thinking.
4. The purpose of a journal is to record and express thoughts to God and then reflect later on how God has worked in your life.

Apply IT!

1. Begin next week and schedule one day dedicated God. Determine beforehand what you will do on your day with the Lord.
2. When God speaks to you this week, write down those impressions in a journal. Direct your thoughts to God.
3. Review your journal at the end of the week.

How to Coach Someone Using this Material

Many churches will teach this material in a group setting. This is the normal way to use the material, but it's not the only way. If you choose to teach a group of people, outlines and PowerPoints are provided for all five equipping books on a CD. You may purchase this CD at www.joelcomiskeygroup.com or by calling 1-888-344-CELL.

Another way to train someone is to allow the person to complete each lesson individually and then ask someone of the same gender to coach him or her. The coach would hold the "trainee" responsible to complete the lesson and share what he or she is learning.

I believe in multiple methods for teaching material. The fact is that not everyone can attend group-training meetings. But the person still needs training. Coaching is a great option.

Coaching the trainee through the material

Ideally, the coach will meet with the trainee after each lesson. At times, however, the trainee will complete more than one lesson and the coach will combine those lessons when they meet together.

The coach is a person who has already gone through the material and is now helping someone else in the training process. Additionally a coach must have:

- a close walk with Jesus.
- a willing, helpful spirit. The coach doesn't need to be a "teacher." The book itself is the teacher—the coach simply holds the trainee accountable with asking questions and prayerful encouragement.

I recommend my book, *How to be a Great Cell Group Coach*, for additional understanding of the coaching process (this book can also be purchased on the CCS web site or by calling 1-888-344 CELL). The principles in *How to be a Great Cell Group Coach* apply not only to coaching cell leaders but also to coaching a trainee. I recommend the following principles:

- Receive from God. The coach must receive illumination from Jesus through prayer so he has something of value to give to the trainee.

- Listen to the person. The coach's job is to listen to the trainee's answers. The coach should also listen to the trainee's joys, struggles, and prayer concerns.

- Encourage the trainee. Often the best thing the coach can do is point out areas of strength. I tell coaches to be fanatics for encouragement. We all know our failures and have far too much condemnation hanging over us. Encouragement will help the trainee press on and look forward to each lesson. Try to start each lesson by pointing out something positive about the person or about what he or she is doing.

- Care for the person. The person might be struggling with something above and beyond the lesson. The material might bring out that specific problematic area. The best coaches are willing to touch those areas of deep need through prayer and counsel. And it's one hundred percent acceptable for the coach to simply say, "I don't have an answer for your dilemma right now, but I know someone who does." The coach can then go to his or her own coach to find the answer and bring it back the next week.

- Develop/train the person. Hopefully the person has already read the lesson. The goal of the coach is to facilitate the learning process by asking specific questions about the lesson.

- Strategize with the trainee. The coach's job is to hold the trainee accountable to complete the next lesson and/or finish the current one. The coach's main role is to help the trainee sustain the pace and get the most out of the material.

- Challenge the person. Some think that caring is good but confronting is wrong. The word care-fronting combines the two and is what the Bible promotes. If we truly care, we'll confront. The Spirit might show you areas in the trainee's life that need to come under the Lordship of Christ. The best approach is to ask for permission. You might say, "Tom, may I have permission to speak to you about something I'm noticing?" After the person gives you permission, you can then tell him what the Lord is laying on your heart.

First session

When the coach meets with the trainee, the Holy Spirit will guide the session. Creativity and flexibility should reign. I do recommend, however, the following principles:

- Get to know the person. A great way to start is to use the Quaker questions. This will help you to warm up to each other. After the first week, the coach can open in prayer and simply ask about the trainee's life (e.g., family, work, studies, spiritual growth, etc.)

> ### Quaker questions
> 1. Where did you live between the ages of 7–12?
> 2. How many brothers and sisters did you have?
> 3. What form of transportation did your family use?
> 4. Whom did you feel closest to during those years?

- Be transparent. Since you've already completed this training material, share your experiences with the trainee. Transparency goes a long way. Great coaches share both victories and struggles.

"Coaching questions" to use each week

A great coach asks lots of questions and listens intently. The goal is to draw the answers from the trainee so that he or she applies the material to daily living. Key questions to ask each time are:

1. What did you like best about the lesson(s)?
2. What did you like least about the lesson(s)?
3. What did you not understand?

4. What did you learn about God that you didn't know previously?
5. What do you personally need to do about it?

The coach doesn't have to ask each of the above questions, but it is good to get into a pattern, so the trainee knows what to expect each week.

Pattern to follow each week

1. Prepare yourself spiritually before the session begins.
2. Read the lesson in advance, remembering the thoughts and questions you had when you went through the material.
3. Start the session in prayer.
4. Ask the coaching questions.
5. Trust the Holy Spirit to mold and shape the trainee.
6. Close in prayer.

Index

Q

Quaker, 83
quality, 8, 20, 23, 25, 42
Quiet time, 9, 16, 20, 31, 69
quiet time, 5, 9, 9, 10, 12, 13, 14, 15,
        16, 17, 18, 19, 20, 21, 22, 23,
        25, 28, 30, 32, 29, 25, 15, 22,
        33, 32, 39, 46, 60, 35, 36, 38,
        42, 44, 46, 48, 49, 50, 51, 52,
        53, 54, 56, 57, 59, 63, 67, 68,
        70, 78, 71, 76

R

relationship, 9, 10, 24, 2, 41, 47, 15,
        46, 79
reward, 8, 14, 15, 33, 35, 36, 66
room, 9, 14, 15

S

Sabbath, 71, 79
Satan's voice, 43
schedule, 15, 17, 18, 19, 20, 21, 17,
        23, 25, 18, 20, 21, 23, 25, 19
secret places, 28
seeking God, 32, 35, 36
Seoul, Korea, 53
silence, 27, 42, 44, 48
specific place, 8
specific time, 8, 9, 25
spiritual, , 84
spiritual food, 13

T

tameon, 28
telephone, 28
Time with God, 10

U

Unhindered communion, 50

W

weakness, 32
Will of God, 56

Worship, , 46, 47, 48, 49, 51

Y

Yoido Full Gospel Church, 53